Piano Exam Pieces

ABRSM Grade 6

Selected from the 2013 & 2014 syllabus

Name

Date of exam

GW00370591

Contents

Editor for ABRSM: Richard Jones

		page
LIST A		
1	**Johann Sebastian Bach** Invention No. 14 in B flat, BWV 785	2
2	**Jan Ladislav Dussek** Rondo: second movement from Sonatina in E flat, Op. 19 No. 6	4
3	**Johann Christoph Kellner** Fugue: No. 2 from Six Fugues	8
LIST B		
1	**Johannes Brahms** Waltz in A flat: No. 15 from Waltzes, Op. 39	10
2	**Enrique Granados** Danza de la rosa: No. 3 from *Escenas poéticas*, Series 1	12
3	**Robert Schumann** Fürchtenmachen: No. 11 from *Kinderscenen*, Op. 15	14
LIST C		
1	**Lennox Berkeley** Allegro: No. 5 from *Five Short Pieces*, Op. 4	16
2	**Jason Rebello** A Wise Bud	18
3	**Trad. Chinese** Jingpo shan ge, arr. Zhang Zhao	20

Other pieces for Grade 6

LIST A

4 **T. Arne** Presto: 1st movt from Sonata No. 7 in A. Thomas Arne, *8 Keyboard Sonatas* (Faber)

5 **Haydn** Andante in D: No. 1 from *Différentes petites pièces faciles et agréables*. Haydn, *Klavierstücke, Klaviervariationen* (Henle) or Haydn, *Différentes petites pièces* (Edition HH)

6 **D. Scarlatti** Sonata in C minor, Kp. 11 (L. 352). Scarlatti, *2 Sonatas* (Bärenreiter) or No. 3 from Scarlatti, *200 Sonatas*, Vol. 1 (Editio Musica Budapest)

LIST B

4 **Beethoven** Andante: 2nd movt from Sonata in G, Op. 79. Sonata published individually (ABRSM) or Beethoven, *The 35 Piano Sonatas*, Vol. 3 (ABRSM)

5 **Chopin** Mazurka in A flat (op. posth., KK IVb No. 4). No. 57 from Chopin, *Mazurkas* (Peters or Henle)

6 **S. Heller** Etude in D, Op. 46 No. 8. *More Romantic Pieces for Piano*, Book 4 (ABRSM)

LIST C

4 **Valerie Capers** Mr 'Satchmo': No. 8 from *Portraits in Jazz* (OUP)

5 **Ibert** La cage de cristal: No. 8 from *Histoires* (piece published individually: Leduc) or Ibert, *Quatre pièces célèbres extraites des Histoires* (Leduc)

6 **Huw Warren** Open. *Elena Riu's R&B Collection* (Boosey & Hawkes)

First published in 2012 by ABRSM (Publishing) Ltd,
a wholly owned subsidiary of ABRSM, 24 Portland
Place, London W1B 1LU, United Kingdom
© 2012 by The Associated Board of the Royal
Schools of Music

Music origination by Julia Bovee
Cover by Kate Benjamin & Andy Potts
Printed in England by Headley Brothers
Ltd, The Invicta Press, Ashford, Kent

FSC
www.fsc.org
MIX
Paper from
responsible sources
FSC™ C109619

Invention No. 14 in B flat

BWV 785

J. S. Bach
(1685–1750)

In 1722–3 Bach entered 30 newly composed pieces into the *Clavierbüchlein* (Little Keyboard Book) for his young son Wilhelm Friedemann. The first 15, each entitled 'Praeambulum', were in two contrapuntal parts, and the second 15, each entitled 'Fantasia', in three parts. Shortly afterwards, in early 1723, he wrote out a fair copy of the 30 pieces, bringing them into their definitive form. The two-part pieces were now entitled 'Inventio' (Invention), and the three-part pieces 'Sinfonia'; they were presented in a new key order and the music text was thoroughly revised. According to the new title-page, the Inventions and Sinfonias were designed to foster good playing in two and three parts, to help students to invent and develop good musical ideas, and above all 'to arrive at a *cantabile* style of playing and acquire a strong foretaste for composition'.

The B flat Invention, selected here, is essentially monothematic, like most of the Inventions. It is based on a decorated broken-chord theme, which is followed immediately by its own inversion. The witty play on direct and inverted forms of the theme that ensues is one of the main sources of the piece's attractiveness. Dynamics are left to the player's discretion.

Source: autograph fair copy, 1723, Staatsbibliothek zu Berlin, Preussischer Kulturbesitz, Mus.ms.Bach P610

Rondo

Second movement from Sonatina in E flat, Op. 19 No. 6

J. L. Dussek
(1760–1812)

Jan Ladislav Dussek was a Bohemian composer and keyboard virtuoso who had an international career, being active at various times in Germany, France, England, the Netherlands, Russia and Lithuania, as well as in his native Bohemia. During his London period (1789–99) he became a fashionable piano teacher, set up a music publishing business with his father-in-law, and performed on several occasions with Haydn, who commented on his 'remarkable talents'.

In this Rondo, the central subdominant episode (bb. 29–44) might be articulated like the rondo theme itself (cf. bb. 1 and 29), though perhaps with a lighter staccato. The first edition of the Six Sonatinas, Op. 19, contains many errors, and in this movement it has proved necessary to correct numerous details without comment.

Source: *Six sonatines pour le fortepiano ou le clavecin*, Op. 19 (London: Longman & Broderip, *c*.1792)

Fugue

No. 2 from Six Fugues

J. C. Kellner
(1736–1803)

The German organist Johann Christoph Kellner was the son of Johann Peter Kellner, a friend and colleague of J. S. Bach. He studied both with his father and with Georg Benda. Later he became court organist in Kassel, as well as cantor at the Lutheran Church. He composed much keyboard music, both in the fashionable *galant* style of his day and in a more traditional contrapuntal style, as in the collection of six fugues from which this piece is selected.

This lively three-part fugue falls into three paragraphs. The first paragraph is the exposition containing soprano, alto and bass subject entries; it closes in b. 10 in the dominant key of G. In the middle paragraph there are two- and three-part stretto (overlapping) entries; the music modulates to the relative minor, A, and then returns via the circle of fifths to the tonic key at b. 25. The concluding paragraph is in the tonic key throughout, and occasional subject entries alternate with new episodes, mostly based on the triadic head-motif of the subject.

In b. 31, right hand, first quaver, the source has a quaver *e*, which appears to be wrong and has been replaced by an editorial quaver rest. Dynamics are left to the player's discretion.

Source: *Six fugues pour les orgues ou le clavecin* (The Hague: B. Hummel, n.d.)

B:1

Waltz in A flat

No. 15 from Waltzes, Op. 39

Johannes Brahms
(1833–97)

The waltz, a dance for couples in triple time, has enjoyed the longest popularity among all modern ballroom dances. It grew out of South German or Austrian country dances known as *deutsche Tänze* (German Dances) and became popular throughout Europe in the late 18th and early 19th centuries. By the time Brahms began visiting Vienna regularly during the 1860s, the vogue for the Viennese waltz, cultivated above all by the Strauss family, was at its height, and Brahms greatly admired the waltzes of his friend Johann Strauss, Jr.

Brahms's 16 Waltzes, Op. 39, composed in 1865 and published in the following year, were originally written for piano duet, but the composer later arranged them for solo piano. The Waltz in A flat, selected here, has always been the most celebrated of the entire collection. The grace notes in bb. 3, 17, and 31 are to be played before the beat. The composer's left-hand markings (arpeggio, staccato, or neither) are best adhered to precisely – Brahms was a stickler for accuracy of detail and no doubt intended the variety of touch.

Adapted from *A Keyboard Anthology*, Second Series, Book 4, edited by Howard Ferguson (ABRSM)

Danza de la rosa

No. 3 from *Escenas poéticas*, Series 1

Enrique Granados
(1867–1916)

Danza de la rosa Dance of the Rose; **Escenas poéticas** Poetic Scenes

Enrique Granados was essentially self-taught as a composer. From 1890 onwards he established a reputation as a concert pianist, and in 1901 he founded his own music school, the Academia Granados, in his native city of Barcelona. In 1916, during the First World War, he was crossing the English Channel when his ship was torpedoed, and he lost his life in a futile attempt to save his wife.

Granados's musical style fuses elements of the 19th-century Romantic tradition with the idioms of Spanish folk music. He is regarded as one of the founders of the modern indigenous school of Spanish piano music. The first of two sets of *Escenas poéticas*, from which this piece is selected, dates from 1912.

The pedalling given here reproduces that of the original edition. All grace notes are best played before the beat.

© 1996 by The Associated Board of the Royal Schools of Music
Adapted from *A Romantic Sketchbook for Piano*, Book 5, edited by Alan Jones (ABRSM)

Fürchtenmachen

No. 11 from *Kinderscenen*, Op. 15

Edited by Howard Ferguson

Robert Schumann
(1810–56)

Fürchtenmachen Frightening; **Kinderscenen** Scenes from Childhood

This is one of 13 piano pieces that Robert Schumann collectively entitled *Kinderscenen*. They were written in 1838 in the midst of a five-year period when Schumann devoted himself exclusively to the composition of piano music and wrote some of his greatest works for the instrument.

'Fürchtenmachen' is constructed in rondo form (ABACABA). The rondo theme A (bb. 1–8) establishes a mood of foreboding. Then, in the faster episodes B and C (bb. 9 and 21) we can imagine that frightening incidents take place.

The metronome mark is the composer's. The *con Ped.* marking at the beginning indicates that the sustaining pedal is to be used wherever required. **In the exam, all repeats should be observed.**

Source: first edition, *Kinderscenen. Leichte Stücke für das Pianoforte*, Op. 15 (Leipzig: Breitkopf & Härtel, *c.*1838)

Allegro

No. 5 from *Five Short Pieces*, Op. 4

Lennox Berkeley
(1903–89)

The English composer Lennox Berkeley studied languages at Oxford University, but later went on to study composition with Nadia Boulanger in Paris (1927–32), where he made the acquaintance of Poulenc and Stravinsky. He taught at the Royal Academy of Music from 1946 to 1968. In the 1920s he composed in the neoclassical style that was current at the time, but he later developed a more romantic turn of phrase.

The *Five Short Pieces*, Op. 4, were first published in 1937. The last of them, reproduced here, is a lively, light-hearted piece, notable for its sudden shifts of key and its irregular metre.

AB 3633

C:2

A Wise Bud

Jason Rebello
(born 1969)

Jason Rebello is trained as both a classical and jazz musician, and has worked with artists such as Sting, Jeff Beck and Wayne Shorter, as well as the Hallé Orchestra. Stuart Nicholson, author of *Jazz: the Modern Resurgence*, said of him: 'In terms of sheer ability and potential, Jason is probably the finest young jazz musician this country has produced. His [piano] playing has great poise and maturity, which is unusual in somebody so young.'

This piece was commissioned by ABRSM, and is dedicated to and inspired by the jazz pianist Earl Rudolph 'Bud' Powell, born in the USA in 1924. The composer has written: 'Powell is one of the most influential pianists in the jazz style known as bebop. Although this piece is notated, the important element in jazz is improvisation. Musicians such as Bud Powell and Charlie Parker were skilled improvisers with an ability to create new melodies on existing chord structures. It is worth listening to Bud's recordings to get the feel of how this piece should be played.' Dynamics are left to the player's discretion.

景颇山歌

Jingpo shan ge

Arranged by Zhang Zhao

Trad. Chinese

Jingpo shan ge Jingpo Folksong

This piece belongs to the folk music of the Jingpo minority, an ethnic group which centuries ago settled in the province of Yunnan in south-west China, on the border with Burma. The Jingpo have their own language, which belongs to the Tibetan-Burmese family of tongues. They are known for their independence, fighting skills, and social grouping in clans.

In this folksong arrangement, the sustaining pedal is often called for where three hands would otherwise be required (e.g. bb. 9–10). For the same reason, the pedal is needed in bb. 66–73. In b. 19 etc. it is convenient to put the left hand over the right.

© People's Music Publishing House, Beijing